Hey, Are You...Magnetic?

The Currency of Life

by   *Philip Spruce*

Foreword

Proverbs 18:21: "The power of life and death is in the tongue…"

Matthew 6:22: "The eye is the lamp of the body. So, if your eye is healthy, your whole body will be full of light…"

Intro

Firstly, I would like to say that this is not a religious book, although if you use it religiously that would be good for you. I do attest to the existence of God, or Goddess, but I do not specifically claim a religion, although the essence of what I'm saying is at the heart of all religions...

Did you know that your perception can literally alter the things around you? Of course, we have all heard that the state of your mind controls your life, therefore if you change your thoughts change you your life etc., but did you actually know there is scientific proof to back this up?

On a quantum level, quantum meaning sub-atomic, or the things that make up atoms (electrons, protons, and neutrons) and beyond that, your gaze, depending on the contents of your mind, can rearrange the electrons of the things it hits upon; just as when you look at someone, you can make them feel shy or nervous depending on what you're emitting energetically, your gaze can alter the sub-atomic structure of whatever it's looking at. Both happen at the same time, meaning that when you look at someone as aforementioned, your intent/focused energy is inducing a change in their physiology from a quantum basis to the evolution of the mood that they feel. Everything is always and only affected from the sub-atomic basis, which then trickles down into physicality…

Now imagine when you look at your whole life from an introspective (but no less impactful) 'eye,' the underlying thoughts and attitudes that are buried deep inside you (which are always operating) are literally and subtly expressed via your perception, how you look at the world, and sculpt your external environment with the physical tools of your perception: the eyes…

And so if someone asks you randomly, "hey, are you magnetic?" What are they essentially asking you? Are your eyes sculpting you a desirable reality? Based on healthy thoughts and emotions which constitute your perception, or are you creating or attracting things from an unhealthy 'magnetic' basis, which you could or could not be aware of?

 This is why sometimes we say: "why is this happening to me?" or 'why does life treat me this way? 'Why do I find myself in the same situations over and over again,' etc... We are unaware of the subconscious mechanisms of our being, because we think the conscious-mind is all there is; that is only the tip of the ice-berg. We think life just happens to us for the most part and we can't control a damned thing, but the truth is my friends, (also scientifically speaking), is that we are magnets, whether you like it or not. And most of the time, we are attracting things by default, not consciously. But knowledge can make the difference between you doing this attracting process (called manifestation in esotericism) unconsciously or consciously, the very knowledge that I am about to share with you now. I hope you enjoy harnessing the magnetic power within you by the end of this book.

Table of contents:

_______________________________ *Chapter 1*

In life, we are bound to have a dream; something that we wish to accomplish in this life that would give us grand amounts of passion, fulfillment, and happiness. This could be having the ideal relationship/lover, a business, wanting to do a craft full-time (like acting or making jewelry), or simply a change in personality; let's say you wanted to be more confident, or even humble: affirmations are the bridge that can get you there.

Now what is an affirmation? It is basically a statement that affirms your wish or desire with the confidence and expectation that it's coming, happening, or is already here. For example, if you wanted to be rich one day, but didn't know exactly how you would get there yet, you could simply start saying: "I will be rich one day." This puts the wish in the future tense, so it is not that powerful but it's a good start. Now, if you were to say "I am approaching a state wealth every day," that is more powerful than the former, because you are saying that it is happening; this puts the wish (to become rich) more in the now. If you say, "I am rich already," that is mighty powerful; you have basically collapsed the time it would take significantly. You have said it already happened, so it must happen! (Yes, that's a trick to circumvent your mind's <u>perception</u> of time, particularly the conscious mind. It's a fast-forward button essentially).

So basically, affirmations are accelerants, catalysts to your desire. They make you magnetic to what you want, and when you are magnetic to what you want, you will probably get it faster. It's like when you rub a piece of metal or iron long enough and it becomes magnetic to other metals. Affirmations do the same thing to your mind, but the power comes from the heart. This is because the mind, unlike the heart, has a filter for perception. Raw energy comes from the heart, and it is 100 times more electromagnetically powerful than the mind-brain complex, and this is a scientific fact as well. Emotions have the power, but thoughts guide them.

So if affirmations are accelerants basically, what does that mean practically? It means that you won't have to do as much physical work for what you want. Not all, but not as much, which is considerable and helpful in our time-pressed reality. For example, let's say you wanted a dream car; you know the make, model, color, engine type, speaker system that you want it to have. Instead of painstakingly looking for that car all over for a certain period of time, you can and actually will find it in one of your first four searches, cutting the time in half, just to give you an idea. It all depends on the faith of the person wanting, but when you really want something of course, nothing can stop you, especially time.

How you find it is key too. The difference with finding things when using affirmations is that those things actually find you, because remember, you're magnetic now, meaning that you have a force that's working for you day and night; some call this God, some call this faith, but whatever you call it, know that it is working via a neutral force called magnetism. In finance, this would be considered passive income.

Just like how there is gravity; it (magnetism) operates independently of God and is a thing in and of itself 24/7; it does not deny God. So how your wish finds you (if it's a material thing) is through serendipity via magnetism; it's like a whole team of universal laws and principles comes in to help you once you start having faith (or magnetism).

 Serendipity is the art of finding things when you're not looking for them. You might be out for a cup of coffee one day, and then you see the car in all its grandeur and exactness of your dream for sale parked on the corner. Or you're with your family on vacation, where the intent is to have fun, but you stumble upon a dealership with the car you want for a good deal. Serendipity works with affirmations (and visualizations) naturally. Depending on who you are and your style, you may be more of a visualizer than an affirmer, but if you start to verbalize, you will naturally start to see visions of the thing that you want, like daydreams. But for the purposes of this book, I am sticking to verbalization.

_______________________________________ *Chapter 2*

Ok, so affirmations primarily work through the 'organs' of the brain-mind complex and the heart-emotion complex. I say complex because it is not just the physical aspect of the organ that is functioning; the heart and brain. There is also a spiritual law besides serendipity and magnetism that states: "as above, so below," which means basically that every physical thing has a spiritual or non-visible counterpart/function. The heart also has the emotions to generate besides the duty of pumping blood to every part of your physical body. Hence why certain break-ups have been proven to cause heart-attacks, and why after an old person that was in a long-term relationship dies, the other partner soon follows after. I'm sure you've heard of stories like that. But it's because emotionally, the pain of the loss was too great, and what organ did it attack? The heart. And when someone is stressed out, guess what type of attack tends to happen? Yup you got it, a stroke a.k.a. brain attack and or a heart attack again! The heart shows up twice, alluding to its elementary imposition and influence on everything humane.

Now emotions really give affirmations their prerequisite power, as we can see; when you say an affirmation, for it to be effective, it must be making you feel good or giving you a sense of relief, otherwise don't say it. They must feel naturally contrived from your mind and heart, not forced. For example, I might be able to say some affirmations that you can't simply due to the fact that one: I have a greater amount of faith than you to begin with, and two: it just feels more comfortable to me personally; style is important, and you won't feel good trying to copy someone else's, (possibly). (Sometimes I have borrowed from others' if it really resonated with me, but the key word is resonate).This good feeling is what does the magnetizing work for you; it is the difference between getting what you want or not within a desirable period of time. Without feeling, your efforts are almost dead, you got it? Got it. You might as well go put one-hundred percent physical effort into getting what you want (If it's material things).

 Now after the heart has gotten involved, you grab the steering wheel which is the mind, but the mind is divided into two parts: the conscious and the subconscious, i.e., the masculine and the feminine. The subconscious takes up ninety percent of your mind, leaving ten to the conscious. The former holds your deepest, rawest aspects of self that conscious-mind either filters out or suppresses. It works with more the emotions than logic, which is why it's considered the feminine aspect of your brain.

The conscious mind is the tool your primarily use to navigate your every-day life, mundane things such as counting the change you receive after a monetary transaction, looking before you cross the street, going to work and school because you know you need money or the college degree to get the job that leads to money; the conscious mind works more with logic and ego and is thus considered the masculine aspect of your brain.

And so to add it all together, magnetism is created via the subconscious mind and the heart, via the ignition of the conscious mind. Let me explain. Even though the conscious mind is only ten percent of your brain-mind complex, it still has a significant role, as you could've surmised before: just because it's only used for mundane things doesn't mean that it's unimportant, as the mundane is a part of reality just as much as the spiritual world, and if you choose to ignore the spiritual world, then you better have a supremely functioning conscious mind, which it is safe to say that most of us don't, because we are so longing for emotional fulfillment, which the subconscious mind never lets you forget by the way in conjunction with the heart. Hence, you are reading this book.

The conscious mind is the one that makes the life changing decisions upon analysis (or lack of) from internal and external factors in your world; for example, if there is a problem with your toilet, you will obviously get a plumber to look at it; this is the conscious mind's function. So if you look at your life and see that you are dissatisfied and really unhappy, the conscious mind will make the decision to get help, as it sees your emotional and psychological state is suffering. The conscious mind is also responsible for the commitment aspect and the discipline necessary to maintain the change. Hopefully YOU, which are higher than the mind, which is the substance invisible behind the mind but self-felt nonetheless, will use your conscious mind to get the help you deserve, but that's another story for another day.

So, you make the decision to use affirmations, right? (Hopefully). So, you must consciously say them now; articulate them with the emotions and not just the flexion of the tongue. Once you start saying your affirmations consciously on a regular basis, the weight of them will sink into your subconscious mind cumulatively until they are permanently resting at the bottom like rocks in a river. This is the building-momentum phase, and as we know, once momentum is built, you don't have to pedal your bicycle much...

This will permanently influence your belief system, which is the basis for the kind of magnetism you have, whether good or bad. If you have a negative belief system, you're going to attract shitty things to yourself quite honestly. You'll constantly end up with shitty relationships, partners, jobs, encounters, etc. If you have a positive belief system, the following will occur. And if it's ok, then it's ok. There's many levels between the two extremes, but always make sure you're more toward the positive end…

To clarify just in case some may not know, a belief system is like an explanation for why you do the things you do and why you see things the way you do. It is the justification behind your physical and psycho-emotional behaviors, the programming. For example, most of us (if you are between the ages of 18 and 24) are in school, particularly college, and why? Because from the time we were born, we were enrolled into an institution that taught us the 'rules' of society and basically what is really important in life (rather erroneously): 'a job and money.' And when we looked at the world around us, we could see that indeed, money is important; without it, you'll be the bum on the street, hungry, homeless; you won't even get to do the things you want to do, much less need. Our parents talked about it all the time, even complained about it. The concept of money was so overly verified via all our senses that it became a permanent part of our belief system, our collection of things that we mentally and emotionally value, and express habitually through action; we must get it by some means in our lifetime; how is up to you and goes further into your own personal belief system, which is formed through experience, but most of us still believe that a college a degree is the way to do it. Correct me if I'm wrong in your own mind.

Affirmations basically work on the belief system; they either grind some parts down or completely transform everything, or just a particular aspect, depending on what you're saying. Like I said before for illustrative purposes, if you want confidence, you have to feel like it's in you. You know it as a concept in your intellectual mind, and may have even pretended to come off as confident because you perceive the psycho-social benefits of being so, but because you don't feel it naturally in you, it is not genuinely a part of YOUR belief system that deals with your personal self-esteem. So how do you go about getting it? One, you create a comfortable affirmation that you can handle and feel some relief from; if you did not automatically breathe deeply after saying it, it was not causing any stirring of good emotion within you; better breathing is a bonified physical symptom of a good affirmation; you won't even have to force it.

Once you give this selected affirmation a regiment, say thrice in the morning and thrice at night, and you start to feel the power of it building within you, i.e., you're saying it with more certainty, speed, and belly strength, you'll start to notice that in your everyday life, you're doing things now that you haven't done before. You order your food with more authority, you ask people to kindly but firmly step out of your way if you're walking down the street in New York City. Or wherever you are. You hesitate less to speak your mind. You have now validated the feeling of confidence you created with your affirmations in the real world (the ultimate testing grounds) but you did not do it consciously. You did it subconsciously, i.e., naturally. To do things with pretense creates nervousness if you cannot handle it. When something becomes subconscious or a habit, one doesn't need to think about doing it; it leaks out.

The concept of progression is very crucial when it comes to affirmations. Still using the confidence example, someone with poor confidence naturally would not say from the start, "I am confident." It's just too much for their belief system to register because they consciously and subconsciously know that's so not true (for now). But if they say, "I have decided to be more confident," that according to the subconscious mind is more acceptable, because it feels better, so it'll work with that. The next step could be "My confidence, however little, is increasing day by day." Until that person can finally say, "I am confident!" After a while you won't even have to say it any more, it'll just feel like work. You just say it every once in a while to stay sharp, but most of the work has been done. That's a sign it has permanently been integrated into your subconscious mind.

Now there are better or ideal times to say affirmations. They are in the morning right upon waking up, and at night right before falling asleep. This is because the conscious, remember, the logical aspect of the mind, is right on its way to sleep or is just waking up; either way it's at its weakest. This is important because the conscious mind has a tendency natural to dismiss or rebel or automatically check things that it knows not to be true based on facts it has collected. Fanciful notions are downplayed, dreams are only in the head etc. So once it sees that you're doing affirmations, it basically says "Oh, that's cute, you wanna improve your little confidence? We'll see how that works..." Because it's going through your memory's data bank and it sees that for most of your life, you have not been confident. So it kind of teases you. But you need this resistance initially to give your will-power a work-out. I'm recommending that if you want the least resistance from your conscious mind, say the affirmations when it's at its weakest: in the morning right upon wake, and at night as you feel the zzzz's catching onto you. And say them until you fall asleep; it's the perfect cementation process for the integration of the affirmation. When you are strong enough in it, you can say them throughout the day even.

 Lastly with affirmations, it is not the quantity of times you say it, but the quality of emotion with which you say it. If you want to use affirmations to gain material things, it is easy, but it is only as easy as you feel it is, and that is based on your level of self-esteem believe it or not. That is the key to at least sixty percent of the good and bad things in life. Therefore, take care and good-bye...no I'm just playing; I have taken the privilege of kick-starting your magnetizing journey by creating some good-feeling affirmations for wealth and self-esteem that you can say at your convenience. Some will have the broken down versions and some will not, quite frankly because some things just need to be said as is; you can't figure out a way out of breathing; you will always have to use that diaphragm and suction from either the nose or mouth, and you will be grateful for still choosing to breathe even if you don't feel like it. And in the same way, the emotional oxygen that certain affirmations will give you from saying them unabashedly is still beneficial even if you don't feel like saying them, because their truths are so readily accessible and digestible to your whole being. Like say for instance, "I am deserving of love." Or, "It is good to love." No matter your romantic and non-romantic experiences with love, it will still be yearned for, it will still have healing effects, love-true love-is always medicinal. One can choose to further break down the affirmations I haven't if you feel the need. And on the last note, they have seriously helped my being, and I know they will help yours if you stick to it. Enjoy.

<u>Affirmations for self-esteem</u>:

1. "I am kind to myself in thought and word."

Easier version: "I am kinder to myself in thought and word."

Easiest: "I have decided to be kinder to myself."

2. "I am confident."

Easier: "My confidence is increasing day by day."

Easier: "Slowly but surely, my confidence is increasing."

Easiest: "Confidence is a birth-right."

3. "I deserve the good things in life."

Easier: "It is possible for me to have the good things in life."

Easiest: "I acknowledge that it is nice, even in thought, to have the good things in life."

4. "It is natural to love others just as much as myself."

Easier: "It is possible to give and receive love."

Easiest: "Love makes life worth living, despite its pain-giving qualities as well."

5. "I'm a good person worthy of blessings."

Easier: "I'm a good-enough person, and a higher-power sees that I try."

Easiest: "Goodness is in me, therefore, I can attract some good into my life."

6. "I am highly intelligent."

Easier: "I'm as smart as I can be and reserve the right to become smarter."

Easiest: "Intelligence is something that everyone can increase."

7. "I tend to myself like a garden, growing beautiful things within."

Easier: "I am starting to take care of myself."

Easiest: "Self-care is important."

8. "I am a light unto myself and others."

Easier: "I am aware of the flame within me."

Easiest: "If I am full of darkness, then I can have a lot of light by default."

9. "My life has a purpose, even though I might not know what it is."

Easier: "I am here for a reason."

Easiest: "If something as simple as a chair can have a purpose, then I certainly have one."

10. "I'm going to use where I am to get to where I want to be."

Easier: "There are useful resources even in my given circumstance."

Easiest: "I can see the positive in my life if I try."

11. "I maintain a healthy perception of life."

Easier: "I am slowly cleansing my perception of self and the world around me."

Easiest: "I am making the commitment to adjust my perception for better."

12. "I am a great manager of my internal environment."

Easier: "I watch my thoughts vigilantly."

Easiest: "It is good to filter out my thoughts."

13. "I am learning to be a bright sun unto myself and others."

14. "I am preparing to receive my best and brightest days."

15. "I remember that darkness gives way to light, and that without darkness there can be no light."

16. "I embrace both the negative and positive within myself, but I do not feed the negative."

17. "I am balanced within my energy."

18. "I detach myself from things that do not serve me."

19. "I reject all toxicity."

20. "I am greatness in the making."

21. "The universe conspires in my favor all the time."

22. "I am the love of my life."

Easier: "Love will seek me if I seek it from myself."

Easiest: "If I don't love myself, I will never be fulfilled."

23. "Because of my self-love, people are attracted to me."

24. "No matter how I feel, the sun still rises."

25. "No matter how I feel, my blessings still come."

<u>Affirmations for wealth:</u>

1. "I am wealthy."

Easier: "I am approaching a state of wealth every day."

Easiest: "I dream of abundance, but it's not an unreasonable dream."

2. "Money comes to me naturally."

Easier: "There are many ways to get money, but which one do I want?"

3. "I love what I can do with money."

Easier: "Money makes you limitless in action, and that's what I want."

4. "I am successful in what I choose to do."

Easier: "I am doing what I can to bring me success."

Easiest: "Success is attainable."

5. "I am creating the life that I want."

Easier: "The life that I want is not far from me."

Easiest: "My soul is nourished by glimpses of my dream life."

6. "I believe that the law of attraction works for me."

Easier: "The laws of the universe were meant to guide us and serve us."

7. "I am grateful for the opportunity to change my life using the law

of attraction."

Easier: "I am not afraid to use the leverage that God gives."

Easiest: "If God gave a loop-hole, why not use it?"

8. God can do many things for me if he or she is all powerful."

9. "If I believe and sustain belief, it has been done already."

Easier: "Belief makes everything possible, but sustained belief makes it more probable."

10. "I am set for life."

11. "God adorns me with the blessings I ask for."

12. "God is so abundant he can bless me with a lottery win."

13. "I have more money than I need at all times."

Easier: "The idea of having more money is great."

Easiest: "Who doesn't want a lot of money?"

14. "I am always winning because I learn from my experiences."

15. "The time has come for a change."

16. "Victory is mine."

Easier: "I am working on achieving a victory in all areas of my life."

17. "My blessings are coming to me faster than ever."

Easier: "I can feel the motion of my blessings coming toward me."

18. "My financial desires are building momentum."

Easier: "My wishes are being granted."

Easiest: "I know that God got the message."

19. "I am being patient with my financial status."

20. "I am positive about changing my financial status."

21. "I take divinely guided action toward changing my financial status."

22. "It is normal to have good things."

Easier: "It would be normal to have nice things."

23. "It is normal to have a lot of money."

Easier: "It would be normal to have a lot of money."

24. "In all areas of my life, I am a winner."

Easier: "In all areas of my life, I could win possibly."

25. "I have all that I want abundantly."

Easier: "I look at the good I already have and thank the most high dearly for it."

26. "I love cashing in my lottery ticket."

Easier: "I love the vision of me cashing in my lottery ticket."

Easiest: "It is nice to cash in a lottery ticket, no matter how big or small.

____*Chapter 3: A conclusory reassurance*

My seekers of the better things in life, the hopers and dreamers, even the

realists…this book was meant to be very short and concise. And I assure

you that no book on the law of attraction need be so long and arduous;

these things are never complicated, people are. If after this book you

become more curious on the law of attraction, which will lead you deeper into the arena of metaphysics, the spiritual realm or rather studying it as a science, steer clear of lengthy books. It is truly simple. I have been a victim of such books and so called experts, and the confusion caused thereafter set my manifestation attempts back considerably. If I could sum it up in a sentence, the law of attraction and affirmations' power is basically ask, believe and receive; without these you have nothing to run on, (your magnetism). Some people are good analyzers of the law, but suck in application. This is because they are not practicing it; don't be one of those. Your level of commitment and decisiveness, consistency, is what gets you results with this modality of dealing with life (like anything else), because truly, without self-improvement, the law of attraction will only work against you; if you are actively utilizing it, but not changing the nature of your magnet, you are going to attract even more shit than you would without it. Depends on the level of shit within you, even I still have shit within me, but guess what? It's significantly less, and I'm constantly improving; there's no such thing as perfect, because if there was a ceiling we'd stop improving, and God doesn't want that; he's a rather ambitious person.

So it's all right my friends, we will always make mistakes, though the same kind and nature of the mistakes should change if you are truly learning. Once you harness the power of the subconscious mind together with the conscious, (remember masculine and feminine) you accelerate the learning process. The world wants you to use more of the masculine brain-mind complex, because this is how the world operates; this is how we get things done, mundane things: we wake up at a certain time for work, we complete the work, everything is very calculated and even pre-calculated, but for life to get magical and worth living, we must summon the feminine aspect of ourselves too. This information is known by the elite, and is how they maintain power. The reason why this was not taught in school. If we had learned this from the time we were kids, we would've been where we wanted to be in life by the time we turned 20.

The truth is that we are more of an emotional being than a logical one. We are first a soul, a definite piece of consciousness that God created to have a physical experience here on earth, but he did not intend for us to get disconnected from the source of life. Affirmations strengthen that connection to source via activation of your ethereal body, your counterpart to your physical, which grounds spiritual energy for earthly use; without the ethereal strong, you basically feel very zombie-like, and yes most things in our society tend to dampen the ethereal body; you can think of it as the body that houses intelligence, emotions, the mind, soul, etc., and it's within your physical (the shell). Anyways, the strengthening of this connection to source, or God, as a symptom, will make you more magnetic.

Believe it or not, religious people have a lot of potential magnetism (as by default they continually acknowledge the higher power) but they do not use it actively for what they want, because they think it a sin to ask for material things or use it to pull in material things. It is a trend in some religions if not all to believe that material things are bad for your morality and integrity and all that, but that's where I have to disagree. Lack of abundance, financial especially, causes more evil and crime than being rich. If one is rich, one is less likely to feel malice toward others, be frustrated most of the time subconsciously, which makes you play the blame game more often than not, which leads to learned helplessness and a victim mentality, which bars you from using your personal power to change your life...I'm not saying it's going to solve all your problems, because rich people do tend to kill themselves if they don't find fulfillment, which is the same for all of us, but money does keep certain 'demons' away. No one should have to continually stress about the basics like housing, food, clothing etc. If good people had money, material things like assets, plants, and land, how do you think the world would be? The problem is money in bad hands, so the only cure is good people with money…

 Anything is possible in life, but the power of affirmations makes anything very possible. Use it wisely. "The power of life and death is in the tongue."

____*Tips for using affirmations*

1. Put your right hand over your heart when you're saying your affirmations, like when you say the pledge of allegiance; this sends a message to the subconscious mind that what you are saying is serious and deserves to be in memory. Also, with the right hand on the left chest, act like you are turning the volume up on a radio as you say the affirmation, and see the physiological difference…

2. If you are too shy or not ready yet to say them out loud, start out by writing your affirmations down in a notebook three times each. As you write them, sometimes you may feel like saying them aloud; that's good. That means you are ready to say them or that particular affirmation. This is how I started out, and I still do this method, because sometimes you just don't have the strength to say something you don't quite believe in yet.

3. As you wake up in the morning, it is the best time to say an affirmation, prayer, visualization, whatever floats your boat; this is because the conscious mind (the one that believes in logic, the masculine) is at its weakest. So it will not resist what you are saying a lot, meaning it (the affirmation) will sink down into your subconscious (the feminine one, the one that listens to the heart more) and heart (the all-knowing center of what you truly want and desire and how you really feel about something at any given minute) more easily. At night time the same applies.

4. There is something called a subliminal message, which is a hidden meaning or message in a story, picture, or song or someone's speech, that is conveyed subtly. As you go to sleep, you can listen at low volumes to a subliminal affirmation audio which speaks the affirmations to your subconscious brain gently within the soundscape of the music, if you choose the musical ones. I recommend the ones with the subliminal hidden in the music, and make sure the music is pleasant and something that you like.

5. Binaural beats: these are pure musical tones that are designed to get you into either an alpha, theta, or delta state. If you don't know what those are, those are the progressive stages of sleep/relaxation that you brain enters into, and they are measured in waves. Alpha waves induce

preliminary relaxation. Theta waves initiate you into mid-deep and definite deep sleep. Delta waves mean you're in the clouds now, very deep sleep. Your brain can usually produce/induce these progressive waves on its own, with the help of melatonin and other sleep chemicals that the brain secretes for sleep, but with the stressful state of society, the lives that we live, filled with high-pressure finance goals and unhealthy diets, this is becoming harder for your brain to accomplish. When it comes to affirmations or any re-wiring of the brain, this is extremely important, because the deeper you sleep, the more the brainwashing sinks in and is processed, so to speak. Yes, affirmations are basically a brainwashing process, for your betterment. So, listen to binaural beats as an alternative to saying your affirmations at night (or better yet) after you say them to compound the effectivity. Or, you can even record your own voice and listen to that.

b. Therefore, if you are having problems sleeping, I recommend, though I am not a doctor and you should consult your doctor firstly, that you take some supplements that will help you sleep, such as magnesium, l-tryptophan, iodine, valerian, rhodiola, etc., and they are are natural by the way and work synergistically. I am a proponent of natural things.

6. Of course, among last but not least, close your eyes. The darkness helps with a sense of peacefulness, as in sleep.

7. Know what you want! Don't say something that you do not want, much less ingrain it into your subconscious mind!

8. Try to say your affirmations in the past tense or in the present tense if possible. The past tense is harder to do, but once achieved is so powerful, because it's saying that it already happened (your desire). Present tense indicates that it is happening now. Future tense means that it will happen but you're still giving yourself time to believe in it more, therefore more than likely you will start with that. I did too.

9. Just like you progress with the stages of time: future, present, and past tense, also do the same with the wording of the affirmation. Break it down if you see one that is too hard to say. For example, if you want to say "I love life," but can't say the word love because it is too powerful a reminder of an emotion that you struggle with already, say "I like life," or "I see that on some days I am able to enjoy the simple things in life."

There is no limit to your imagination other than the one you put on it.

Break down, break down, break down!

10. You can actually also say your affirmations during exercise, and even tailor them around exercise! Remember for anything you want you can use affirmations! If you're trying to lift more weights, say "I can lift a thousand pounds." Of course I am exaggerating, but am I? What about, "I am full of testosterone"? Because that's what's needed for muscle mass. "I am full of endurance," "I am benching 500 pounds, etc." And still apply the same rules: progress, break down.